FARMERS

CHRISTINE HONDERS

PowerKiDS press.

Published in 2020 by The Rosen Publishing Group, Inc.
29 East 21st Street, New York, NY 10010

First Edition

Editor: Greg Roza
Book Design: Reann Nye

Photo Credits: Cover, p.1 Africa Studio/Shutterstock.com; pp. 4–22 Abstractor/Shutterstock.com; p. 5 Joshua Resnick/Shutterstock.com; p. 7 Syda Productions/Shutterstock.com; p. 9 NNehring/E+/Getty Images; p. 11 industryviews/Shutterstock.com; p. 13 mailsonpignata/Shutterstock.com; p. 15 symbiot/Shutterstock.com; p. 17 Alaettin YILDIRIM/Shutterstock.com; p. 19 Fotokostic/Shutterstock.com; p. 21 lzf/Shutterstock.com; p. 22 Morsa Images/Taxi/Getty Images Plus/Getty Images.

Library of Congress Cataloging-in-Publication Data

Names: Honders, Christine, author.
Title: Farmers / Christine Honders.
Other titles: Helpers in our community (PowerKids Press)
Description: New York : PowerKids Press, [2020] | Series: Helpers in our
  community | Includes index.
Identifiers: LCCN 2019013737| ISBN 9781725308220 (pbk.) | ISBN 9781725308244
  (library bound) | ISBN 9781725308237 (6 pack)
Subjects: LCSH: Agriculture–Juvenile literature. | Farmers–Juvenile
  literature.
Classification: LCC S519 .H58 2020 | DDC 630–dc23
LC record available at https://lccn.loc.gov/2019013737

Manufactured in the United States of America

CPSIA Compliance Information: Batch #CWPK20. For Further Information contact Rosen Publishing, New York, New York at 1-800-237-9932.

CONTENTS

No Food Without Farmers!

Many years ago, most farmers just grew enough food to feed their family. Today, farmers help feed everyone! Farmers grow plants and raise animals for people to use. They often work day and night, seven days a week. People wouldn't be able to live without farmers!

What Is Farming?

Another word for farming is agriculture. This means the growing of crops and raising of animals for food. Some farmers raise animals that give us **materials** we need to make things we use every day. Farmers don't just grow food. They make our lives better!

History of Farming

Farming allowed early people to settle in one place. This allowed the first towns to grow. People moved there, and some towns grew into cities. Farmers sold their goods to people in cities. New tools, such as tractors, made farming easier and quicker.

Types of Farms

In the United States today, many farms are run by large companies. They grow one kind of crop and sell it to grocery stores or restaurants. They use **technology** to grow crops more cheaply and quickly. In some other countries, more farms are family owned. People live on what they grow.

Fruits, Veggies, and Grains

Farmers may grow fruits, vegetables, or **grains**. They know the right time to plant seeds. They keep the crops watered. They add **fertilizer** to the soil to grow more plants. They **harvest** the crops when they're ripe and ready to sell.

Livestock Farms

Some farmers raise **livestock** for food. These animals include cows, sheep, and pigs. Good livestock farmers keep their animals healthy so our food is safe to eat. Dairy farmers raise cows for milk. Other farmers raise horses so people can ride them.

Farms Touch Everything

Farms give us much more than food. Some grow cotton plants. Some sheep farmers raise sheep for their **wool**. Cotton and wool are used to make clothes and other things. Some farmers grow trees! Trees give us wood with which to make things.

17

To Spray or Not to Spray

Bugs and other things that harm plants are called pests. Some farmers spray pesticides on their crops. Pesticides are **chemicals** that kill the pests. But eating foods with some kinds of pesticides on them can make people sick. Putting chemicals in the air can also harm other plants and animals.

Organic Farms

Organic farms use pesticides too. However, they use pesticides and chemicals from natural sources. Many of these farmers plant different crops every year. This helps keep the dirt healthy and pest-free. Organic farmers feed their livestock organic food as well.

Feeding Your Community and More

Farmers' markets bring farmers close to the community. People can buy fresh fruits and vegetables grown in their area. Farming also creates jobs. Many people depend on farming to make money. Farmers feed our communities at home and all over the world!

GLOSSARY

chemical: Matter that can be mixed with other matter to cause changes.

fertilizer: Something added to soil to help plants grow.

grain: The seeds of some plants that are used for food.

harvest: To gather crops after they've grown.

livestock: Farm animals kept, raised, and used by people.

material: Something from which something else can be made.

technology: The way people do something and the tools they use.

wool: The thick hair of sheep and some other animals.

INDEX

WEBSITES

Due to the changing nature of Internet links, PowerKids Press has developed an online list of websites related to the subject of this book. This site is updated regularly. Please use this link to access the list: www.powerkidslinks.com/HIOC/farmers